HOW TO GUIDE
GIRL SCOUT CADETTES THROUGH

aMAZE!
THE TWISTS AND TURNS
OF GETTING ALONG

IT'S YOUR WORLD — CHANGE IT! A LEADERSHIP JOURNEY

Girl Scouts of the USA

CHAIR, NATIONAL BOARD OF DIRECTORS

Patricia Diaz Dennis

CHIEF EXECUTIVE OFFICER

Kathy Cloninger

EXECUTIVE VICE PRESIDENT, MISSION TO MARKET

Norma I. Barquet

VICE PRESIDENT, PROGRAM DEVELOPMENT

Eileen Doyle

WRITERS: Monica Shah, Mariam McGregor, Alison Hill

CONTRIBUTORS: Jessica Slote, Laura Dobbins, Kate Gottlieb, Toi James, Maja Ninkovic

ILLUSTRATED BY Jennifer Kalis

DESIGNED BY Parham Santana

First published in 2008 by Girl Scouts of the United States of America
420 Fifth Avenue, New York, NY 10018-2798
www.girlscouts.org

ISBN:978-0-88441-716-3

Printed in Italy

4 5 6 7 8 9/16 15 14 13 12 11 10 09 08

Definitions of bullying on page 60 and the statistic on page 63 from Adair, R. and Vyse, L. (2006)
The Role of Bystanders in Bullying: Resource material published by the Anti-Bullying Alliance, London

CONTENTS

"We use our time now to discuss difficult topics—
peer pressure . . . and social problems . . . .
My sincerest wish for these girls is that they are
happy and successful in their later lives and
mostly that they give back to their communities."

—Terri Charest, Girl Scout volunteer, Flower Mound, Texas

AN aMAZing JOURNEY

You are about to guide Girl Scout Cadettes through an amazing maze of a journey, one in which each passageway presents opportunities to navigate personal relationships in the best and most productive ways.

As girls twist and turn through aMAZE, they gain tips and strategies for creating healthy relationships and long-lasting friendships. Ultimately, girls emerge from this maze to *amaze* the world with Take Action Projects that mobilize ever wider circles of people in positive and peaceful interactions. The goal is to increase the peace—one interaction at a time.

How many people does it take to create peace? Well, there are 2.6 million girls in Girl Scouts—and nearly 1 million adults. Peace really could begin with you and the Cadettes.

Coaching Leadership from the Inside Out

Like all Girl Scout leadership experiences, aMAZE is built on the Girl Scout philosophy of leadership, in which girls:

Discover (themselves and their values, and use their knowledge and skills to explore the world),

Connect (care about, inspire, and team with others, locally and globally), and

Take Action (to make the world a better place).

In this way, girls explore leadership from the inside out. As the journey begins, they apply their values to relationships with friends. Then they use those same values to tackle a variety of obstacles to healthy relationships. Finally, they apply what they have learned to take action in the world of relationships around them.

This guide provides you with a wealth of material to coach girls successfully through the passageways of aMAZE. Simply add in your own relationship know-how—and the belief that with your guidance, girls can create more peace in the world—and you're destined for an amazing journey.

Working with the Girls' Book

The girls' book begins with an invitation to the Cadettes to map out the relationship issues that make up the maze of their lives. (You'll engage the girls in a similar activity during your first session together.) The girls' book then moves into information, ideas, and activities on a range of relationship topics.

You'll notice that the sample sessions in this guide parallel these topics and offer activities and discussions specifically designed for a group setting. If the Cadettes are interested in topics or activities from their books that are not incorporated in the sample sessions, go ahead and bring them into the group experience. Familiarizing yourself with the girls' books will make it easy for you to reference activities and sections as needed.

The girls' book encourages the Cadettes to join with friends on various activities, and it provides conversation starters for talking with a trusted adult throughout the journey. Encourage the girls to enjoy these "extras" when, and if, they interest them.

Awards Along the Journey

While journeying through aMAZE, girls have the option of earning three prestigious Girl Scout awards. They can earn one, two, or all three—and they can work toward them as one big team, as mini teams, or individually. The Cadettes can also choose whether to enjoy one ceremony to celebrate earning all the awards or separate ceremonies to mark each award.

Interact Award

This award signifies that girls can advance peace in the world around them—one interaction at a time. To earn it, girls must complete three of the nine challenges listed in the Interact Challenges chart on pages 12–15 of their book—though they can do as many challenges as they like! These challenges, based on topics the girls will explore on the journey, invite the Cadettes to try small—and positive—ways of interacting in their daily lives. For example, one challenge asks girls to invite a new friend to join their established circle. Another asks them to send note cards to acknowledge their friends' admirable qualities.

RECORD AND PASS FORWARD

As the girls finish each challenge, they can use the Interact Challenges chart on pages 12–15 of their book to record their accomplishments and reflect on how "passing it forward" can advance peace in the world.

Diplomat Award

A diplomat "possesses skill or tact in dealing with others." To earn the award, Cadettes demonstrate that they can pass their relationship skills on to others through a Take Action Project. For example, they might teach younger girls how to use "I-Statements" (a skill they will learn in aMAZE) or perform a skit about bullying followed by a discussion of how to cope with bullying. There are more ideas in the girls' book and in this guide, too.

7 STEPS TO TAKING ACTION

To earn the Diplomat Award, it's important for girls to choose and plan their project (as a team or individually) using the seven steps toward Taking Action detailed on page 114 of their book. These steps teach effective planning skills that the girls can use throughout their lives.

Peacemaker Award

Each chapter of the girls' book (and each session when you meet) ends with a "For Your Peacemaker Kit" reflection. This invites the girls to consider how the relationship skills they are exploring could create more peace in the world. Specifically, girls are asked to collect relationship "tools" they can use and pass on to others. The girls earn the Peacemaker Award at the end of the journey by reviewing all the tools they've collected and making a commitment to use them throughout their lives.

Sample Sessions at a Glance

SESSION 1

First Impressions in the Maze

Girls are introduced to the aMAZE journey and:

- identify possible relationship obstacles in the "maze of life"
- identify peers and adults who provide key support in their lives
- make choices and decisions, including a team agreement for the journey
- begin exploring the impact first impressions have on relationships

SESSION 2

Navigating Friendships

Girls start their Peacemaker Kits to collect the relationship skills they practice along the journey, and:

- understand how stereotypes impact relationships
- identify the personal qualities they bring to and seek in healthy friendship circles

SESSION 3

Cliques and Conflicts

Girls identify different types of peer pressure and how it influences them, and:

- practice strategies for managing peer pressure based on values
- understand the exclusive and hurtful behaviors that can happen in cliques
- use "I-Statements" as an important conflict resolution tool

SESSION 4

Caution: Bullies Straight Ahead

Girls identify characteristics of bullying behavior and relational aggression, and:

- practice skills to address bullying behavior and relational aggression
- gain greater understanding of girls' roles as witnesses in bullying situations
- set boundaries and develop strategies for building safe online relationships

SESSION 5

Let Peace Begin with You

Girls explore the Girl Scout definition of leadership and apply it to their lives, and:

- understand how leaders use relationship skills to improve the world

- create and plan a Take Action Project to increase the peace in their world

SESSION 6

Improving Relationships in the World

Girls plan and carry out their Take Action Project, and:

- continue to connect with each other practicing relationship skills individually and as team members

SESSION 7

Toward Peace: Take Action!

Girls complete their Take Action Project, and:

- prepare for the closing ceremony and celebration

SESSION 8

Pass It Forward

Girls evaluate their Take Action Projects, and:

- reflect on their aMAZE journey and their role as leaders who inspire peace through strong, positive relationships

- celebrate their accomplishments

"I love my sixth-grade Girl Scouts.
They are ready to step out and explore all the
world has to offer. Sometimes they lead me."

—Anne-Marie Faul, Girl Scout volunteer, Katy, Texas

YOU AND YOUR GROUP OF GIRL SCOUT CADETTES

Throughout this journey, you and the girls will gain deeper knowledge of one another and the rich traditions of Girl Scouting. So take some time to understand the likes and needs of Cadette-age girls, and then dip into the traditions and ceremonies of Girl Scouts and the "what and how" of creating quality Girl Scout experiences.

As you read about the long-lasting leadership benefits of Girl Scouting, think about your own perspective on leadership and creating peace in the world. Your interest and enthusiasm are sure to be a driving force for the Cadettes as they wind their way through aMAZE.

Understanding Cadette-Age Girls

Girls nearing or in their early teens often feel that everyone and everything around them is changing. Passageways that seemed so clear when they were younger are now fuzzy and filled with obstacles—obstacles that often involve interactions with others. The Cadettes may be looking for new friendships or working to strengthen old ones as they seek out circles where they truly belong. Navigating peer pressure, cliques, and conflicts—and wondering what to do about gossip and bullying, in life and online—may be part of their daily life.

By journeying together through aMAZE, the girls will find they aren't alone when feeling confused or overwhelmed by life's many choices and decisions. By focusing on defining, strengthening, and navigating healthy relationships, they will be able to try out various tactics and mind-sets to improve the relationship dynamics in their lives. They will see that while they can't control all the interactions around them, they can learn to shift their own reactions in order to find the best path for themselves.

Keep in mind that girls in sixth, seventh, and eighth grade:

Feel unique, as if no one else has ever felt the way they do

Display excellent planning skills, long attention spans, and total absorption in their passions (though they may discover a new passion frequently)

Are *extremely* concerned about their friends and peer relationships and put a ton of energy and interest into them (and may develop self-consciousness in front of peers)

Are interested in boys and crushes

Are into "what's hot" and "what's not" in fashion, music, celebrities, and style

Are committed to communicating and getting along with parents/guardians

Feel a lot of pressure from the social scene at school, and think that adults don't understand how complicated their social life is—and how much stress it can cause

Have good communication skills and, with guidance, can present issues effectively in public forums

Like to be with and serve people directly—it's their social nature

COMMUNICATION: IT'S A GOOD THING

Keep families in the loop throughout the journey—and let the girls know you're doing so. This makes communication easy should important issues arise. Keeping an up-to-date list of day and evening phone numbers of the girls' parents, guardians, or caregivers is a good idea, too.

You can also talk with staff at your Girl Scout council about available community resources (university centers, teen help counselors and groups) if specific expertise would be helpful. For example, if girls let you know that relational aggression and other types of bullying (see Session 4) are big issues in their lives, you might want to tap local experts for more insight and support. Schools and local counseling centers, conflict mediation programs, and anti-violence organizations could all be helpful information sources.

FAMILY AND FRIENDS NETWORK

It's great for Cadettes to have a wide network of people in their lives. So reach out and see how parents, aunts, grandmothers, cousins, and other relatives and family friends can be involved in the journey. They might pitch in during the girls' Take Action Project or suggest guest speakers or field trips. They may have a craft expertise to share. Or they may want to assist in planning celebrations and ceremonies—or support the team with transportation and snacks.

What + How: Creating a Quality Experience

I t's not just "what" girls do, but "how" they are engaged that creates a high-quality Girl Scout experience. All Girl Scout experiences are built on three processes that make Girl Scouting unique from school and other extra-curricular activities. When used together, these processes—Girl Led, Cooperative Learning, and Learning by Doing—ensure the quality and promote the fun and friendship so integral to Girl Scouting. Take some time to understand these processes and how to use them with Girl Scout Cadettes.

Girl Led

"Girl led" is just what it sounds like—girls play an active part in figuring out the what, where, when, how, and why of their activities. So coach the girls to lead the planning, decision-making, learning, and fun as much as possible. This ensures that girls are engaged in their learning and experience leadership opportunities as they prepare to become active participants in their local and global communities.

Throughout the journey, you'll find suggestions for ways you can support the girls as they lead discussions and activities. You can also:

• engage the girls in scheduling how often, when, and where the team meets

• encourage them to add on trips and other activities that spark their imaginations

• have them identify topics that matter to them

• have them drive most of the planning, organizing, and implementation of their projects (but you'll want to assist them in thinking through the scale and scope of projects, and guide them to realistic decisions based on their time and resources)

COACHING GIRLS TO LEAD

Tips throughout this guide will help you maximize opportunities for girl leadership. As you delve into the sample sessions, for example, you'll see that you can use the last few minutes of each session to invite girls to volunteer for leadership roles during the next session. Simply have a quick huddle and talk with any girl volunteers about the discussions or activities they want to lead.

Learning by Doing

Learning by Doing, also known as Experiential Learning, is a hands-on learning process that engages girls in continuous cycles of action and reflection that result in deeper understanding of concepts and mastery of practical skills. As they participate in meaningful activities and then reflect on them, girls get to explore their own questions, discover answers, gain new skills, and share ideas and observations with others. Throughout the process, it's important for girls to be able to connect their experiences to their lives and apply what they have learned to their future experiences.

So, for every experience girls have along the journey, encourage time for talking, sharing, reflecting, and applying their insights to new experiences in their lives. As girls lead each other in activities, they will have a chance to practice this approach themselves. Articulating their thoughts and feelings will consolidate what they are discovering about themselves and leadership.

Cooperative Learning

Through cooperative learning, girls work together toward shared goals in an atmosphere of respect and collaboration that encourages the sharing of skills, knowledge, and learning. Working together in all-girl environments also encourages girls to feel powerful and emotionally and physically safe, and it allows them to experience a sense of belonging even in the most diverse groups.

While building their relationship skills, the girls will especially value having a team atmosphere that makes them feel safe and supported. During the first session, you'll partner with the girls on a team agreement. Encourage them to reflect back and speak openly and often about how they are functioning as a team. And although they can do their Take Action Project on their own, they might have more fun creatively working together or in small groups.

Girl Scout Traditions and Ceremonies

Friendship Circles

Even the briefest of ceremonies can take girls away from the everyday to think about hopes, intentions, commitments, and feelings. A ceremony marks a separation from whatever girls have just come from (school, work, dance class, math club) and creates the sense that what will happen now is special and important. So find out how and when girls want ceremonies.

Ceremonies can be as simple as gathering in a friendship circle, lighting a candle, and saying to oneself—or sharing—one hope or affirmation, or reflecting together on one line of the Girl Scout Law. Or girls might read poems, play music, or sing songs. Invite them to create their own simple ways to mark their time together as special (some ideas are offered in Session 1, pages 34–35).

SWAPS

Trading SWAPS (Special Whatchamacallits Affectionately Pinned Somewhere) is a beloved Girl Scout tradition of exchanging small keepsakes. It started long ago when Girl Scouts and Girl Guides from England first gathered for fun, song, and making new friends. Swaps are still a fun way for Girl Scouts to meet and promote friendship. Each swap offers a memory of a special event or a particular girl. A swap usually says something about a Girl Scout's group or highlights something special about where she lives. And it's simple—it could be made from donated or recycled goods.

Health, Safety, and Well-Being

SAFETY-WISE

Keep this Girl Scout reference handy. It details the safety net provided for girls in Girl Scouting. Use it along with any additional information from your council to plan trips and outdoor activities, and to promote the well-being of the Cadettes every time you get together.

The emotional and physical safety and well-being of girls is of paramount importance in Girl Scouting. Look out for the safety of girls by following *Safety-Wise* when planning all gatherings and trips, and:

- checking into any additional safety guidelines your Girl Scout council might have based on local issues

- talking to girls and their families about special needs or concerns

- creating a safe and trusting emotional space for girls by partnering with them to make and stick to a team agreement

- reminding girls not to disclose their names, addresses, or contact information when interacting online

- calling on your council if you need additional expertise or referrals to community resources

Welcoming Girls with Disabilities

Girl Scouts embraces girls with many different needs at all age levels, and with a very specific and positive philosophy of inclusion that benefits all. Each girl is an equal and valued member of a group with typically developing peers.

As an adult volunteer, you have the chance to improve the way society views girls with disabilities. One way to start is with language. Your words have a huge impact on the process of inclusion. People-First Language puts the person before the disability:

CONTACT INFO FOR YOUR GIRL SCOUT COUNCIL

Name: _____

_____

Can help with: _____

_____

_____

_____

Phone: _____

E-mail: _____

_____

SAY	INSTEAD OF
She has autism.	She's autistic.
She has an intellectual disability.	She's mentally retarded.
She has a learning disability.	The girl is learning-disabled.
She uses a wheelchair.	She is wheelchair-bound.
She has a disability.	She is handicapped.

Learn What a Girl Needs

Probably the most important thing you can do is to ask the individual girl or her parents or guardians what she needs to make her experience in Girl Scouts successful. If you are frank and accessible to the girl and her parents, it's likely they will respond in kind, creating a better experience for all.

It's important for all girls to be rewarded based on their best efforts—not completion of a task. Give any girl the opportunity to do her best and she will. Sometimes that means changing a few rules or approaching an activity in a more creative way. Here are a few examples:

• Invite a girl to perform an activity after observing others doing it first.

• Ask the girls to come up with ideas for how to adapt an activity.

Often what counts most is staying flexible and varying your approach.

For a list of online resources, visit www.girlscouts.org and search on "disability resources."

aMAZING Snacks

Food is a great way to bring people together—and, of course, it offers an energy boost. Talk to girls about their snack plans for gatherings. Try experimenting with snack treats that are festive and uplifting: low-fat cheese on wheat crackers, a pitcher of cold water with slices of orange floating in it, herbal iced tea, carrots with yogurt dip, hummus on pita. Think globally and the options will be endless. The team can have fun trying to snack smart as they wind their way through aMAZE.

Understanding the Journey's Leadership Benefits

Though filled with fun and friendship, aMAZE is designed to give girls the tips and strategies they need to develop healthy relationships. "Girls develop healthy relationships" is one of 15 national leadership outcomes, or benefits, of the New Girl Scout Leadership Experience. Experiences in this journey are designed to enable sixth-, seventh- and eighth-grade girls to achieve seven of these outcomes, as detailed in the chart on the next page. You can notice the "signs" of these benefits throughout the journey.

Each girl is different, so don't expect them all to exhibit the same signs to indicate what they are learning along the journey. What matters is that the Cadettes are developing leadership skills and qualities they can use right now—and throughout their lives.

For definitions of the outcomes and the signs that Girl Scout Cadettes are achieving them, see the chart on the next page or *Transforming Leadership: Focusing on Outcomes of the New Girl Scout Leadership Experience (GSUSA, 2008).* Keep in mind that the intended benefits to girls are the cumulative result of traveling through an entire journey—and everything else girls experience in Girl Scouting.

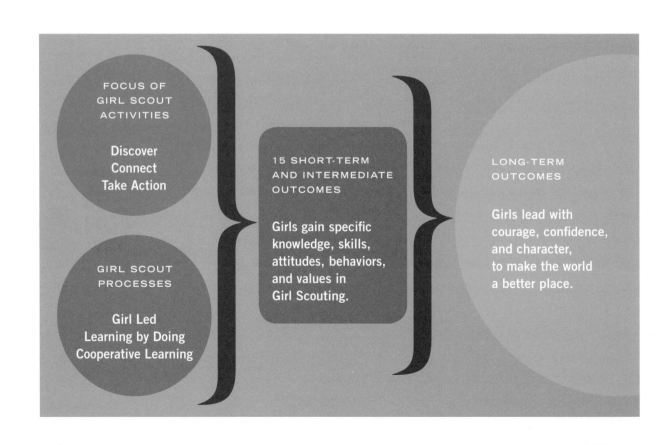

FOCUS OF GIRL SCOUT ACTIVITIES

Discover
Connect
Take Action

GIRL SCOUT PROCESSES

Girl Led
Learning by Doing
Cooperative Learning

15 SHORT-TERM AND INTERMEDIATE OUTCOMES

Girls gain specific knowledge, skills, attitudes, behaviors, and values in Girl Scouting.

LONG-TERM OUTCOMES

Girls lead with courage, confidence, and character, to make the world a better place.

NATIONAL LEADERSHIP OUTCOMES

		AT THE CADETTE LEVEL, girls...	SAMPLE "SIGN" When the outcome is achieved, girls might...	EXAMPLES of how the outcome plays out in this journey
DISCOVER	**Girls develop a strong sense of self.**	are better able to negotiate the effects of sociocultural factors, gender issues, and stereotyping/bias on their sense of self.	make use of strategies to resist peer pressure (e.g., communicate with confidence, take responsibility for own actions).	Sessions 1-3
	Girls develop critical thinking.	are better able to examine issues and ideas from various perspectives.	debate or discuss various perspectives on an issue they are concerned about (e.g., women's rights, global warming).	Sessions 1-3
	Girls develop healthy relationships.	are able to use positive communication and relationship-building skills.	give examples of behaviors they use to promote mutual respect, trust, and understanding.	The entire journey!
CONNECT	**Girls can resolve conflicts.**	strengthen their conflict resolution and prevention strategies.	say how they manage their emotions (e.g., anger, hurt) to diffuse a conflict situation (e.g., don't lose their temper).	Taking on issues and meeting others in the community while planning and taking action.
	Girls feel connected to their communities, locally and globally.	strengthen existing relationships and seek to create new connections with others in their communities	use various ways to connect with others, locally and globally (e.g., the Internet, get-togethers, *destinations*, events).	All steps to the Interact Award
TAKE ACTION	**Girls are resourceful problem solvers.**	increasingly seek out community support and resources to help achieve their goals.	identify people/organizations in their communities to help on some aspect of their project (e.g., obtain editing guidance for media projects).	All steps to the Diplomat Award
	Girls educate and inspire others to act.	show increased commitment to educate others on how to better their communities.	organize a show-and-tell for younger Girl Scouts to educate them about how to be more active in community affairs.	All steps to the Peacemaker Award

Your Perspective on Leadership

The Girl Scout Leadership philosophy—Discover, Connect, Take Action—implies that leadership happens "from the inside out." In Girl Scouts, a leader is not simply someone in a position of authority or someone who likes to be in charge. A leader works collaboratively with others to make things better for everyone.

Your beliefs and values, and your attitude, will likely be a strong influence on the girls. So take time to think about your own leadership philosophy. Try the following reflection exercise and revisit it periodically throughout the journey. You may even find it useful to network with fellow volunteers and share ideas about your progress guiding girls through aMAZE.

Discover	**+**	Connect	**+**	Take Action	**=**	Leadership

DISCOVER

What are some of the values you have that fuel your beliefs about human relationships? How do you strive to set aside your own first impressions or stereotypical thinking when you interact?

_____

_____

_____

_____

What do you want to pass on to girls? What might you not want to pass on to girls?

_____

_____

_____

_____

CONNECT

Think about the healthiest relationships and friendships you have. What skills do you use to create and sustain them?

_____

_____

_____

Have you ever been really pleased with how you resolved a conflict or responded to bullying or peer pressure? How will you use these skills and experiences to guide girls to strengthen their own relationships?

_____

_____

_____

How and when in your life have you experienced the power of truly belonging? What aspects of those experiences can you encourage girls to build into their team?

_____

_____

_____

TAKE ACTION

You are taking action as a volunteer in service to girls. Why? What motivates you to volunteer your time? What impact do you hope to have on girls?

_____

_____

_____

How can you coach girls to create a Take Action Project that truly matters to them and enables them to "pass forward" ideas for more peaceful interactions in their world?

_____

_____

_____

"I like the fact that the girls can come to our meetings and feel comfortable and secure; they are not afraid to speak their minds. I am amazed at the comments they make regarding school and teachers and issues they face."

—Connie A. Fratianni, Girl Scout volunteer and alumna, Manhasset, New York

THE JOURNEY'S 8 SAMPLE SESSIONS

This guide provides a sample schedule for an eight-session journey, with each session lasting about 75-90 minutes. You'll probably find that each sample session offers more than you and the girls will cover in that time. That's perfectly fine because how you decide to work with the sample sessions will be influenced by the girls' input and basic logistics, such as how much time the girls want to spend on the journey overall and whether they want to add on trips or other activities.

During your first gathering, partner with the girls to customize the journey to suit their needs and interests (see page 34 for possible discussion prompts). You may find that the girls want to extend a particular activity or move through some activities quickly and linger over others. As you get to know your group of Cadettes, you'll be able to customize what you do and the time you spend on each activity even further.

Stretching Out the Journey

If the team has time, you might stretch the journey beyond eight sessions. In fact, you may find that that one session can become three. But if you are on a tight schedule, simply engage the girls in the topics they most want to cover in each session. Either way, the goal is for you and the Cadettes to have a meaningful journey. So try to build in time all along the way for the Cadettes to just hang out together, enjoying the safe space and emotional connections so important to girls at this age—and so much a part of what makes Girl Scouting unique.

As time permits, you might want to try some "detours" and add-ons, including:

Trips and Team-Building Activities

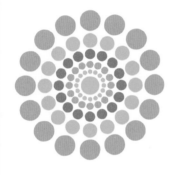

Depending on your location and the season, a visit to a corn maze, hedge maze, rock labyrinth, or other life-size maze will add life-size richness to the journey. (And it's a great excuse for the girls to sightsee, shop, and eat—in other words, have some fun *their* way.)

While visiting a "real" maze, consider adding a team-building challenge to the experience. Girls could pair up and lead each other through the maze while blindfolded, or they could travel through the maze backwards. A short discussion about trust and its give-and-take in relationships would be a great way to round out the experience.

No maze in your region? Create one! The team (and the Family and Friends Network) could set up a mazelike obstacle course—it will give girls the sense of progressing through a series of challenges, and they can do it in pairs or as a team.

Field trips are also a great way to spark the girls' imaginations, especially about choosing a Take Action Project. Visits to local organizations with antiviolence or conflict-mediation programs are sure to fuel any ideas the Cadettes have about "spreading the peace."

Retreats

A weekend away from it all (maybe even at a Girl Scout camp) is a great way for girls to engage in the discussions and role playing that await them in aMAZE. The more relaxed the girls are, the more they'll dive into the relationship obstacles they encounter in the maze of life.

Movie Nights

Many of the relationship topics addressed in this journey are poignantly portrayed (though sometimes exaggerated) in contemporary and classic films. Movie and discussion nights are a great way for girls to sample the many passageways of aMAZE. Girls might even want to partner up with other Cadette groups in the area for mega movie nights.

Fresh Perspectives

Hearing about the experiences of older girls and women can add fresh perspectives to the knowledge Cadettes gain through aMAZE. You don't need to look very far to expand the horizons of middle schoolers. They respect high school girls, so you might invite Girl Scout Seniors and Ambassadors, or other teen community members, to present their own insights on the journey's relationship topics (it's also a chance for the older teens to develop their leadership skills). Your community may have experts in conflict mediation, networking strategies, or other relationship-building skills that you can tap as well.

Creative Stuff

Girls who like to make things—crafts, foods, DIY ("Do It Yourself") projects, inventions, videos—will enjoy sharing their talents with the team. So encourage the girls to share their "favorite to-do's" with each other. They can even give each other something they make, which puts an aMAZing twist on their creativity!

MAKING MEMORIES

If the Cadettes want to create a visual record of any activity along the journey, encourage them to bring to the sessions their cameras, video cameras, or cell phones with picture/video capability. Their books end with a series of journal pages where they can record their thoughts and also archive any "visual memories."

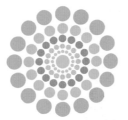

PREPARE AHEAD

Ahead of each meeting with the Cadettes, you'll find it useful to read through the sample session, or the revised session you have developed in partnership with the girls. Thinking about the session as a whole lets you concentrate on the potential impact of each discussion and activity. At the start of sessions, you'll see handy "Advance Prep" tips. Some involve material preparations; others relate to session topics and offer ideas about how to approach them with the girls. Following these tips will ensure that you're ready to guide girls forward in a fun and fresh way.

KEEP BASIC MATERIALS HANDY

A box or bag with markers, pens, scrap paper, glue, scissors, and masking tape will prove handy to bring to the sessions. Perhaps girls and their families can help round up these basic supplies—leftovers will do. If your meeting space has a blackboard or newsprint and easel you can use, that's great. Otherwise, you might want to have a few poster boards or sheets of newsprint handy. Don't invest in anything expensive—recycle file folders, use the back of posters, and so on. A few sessions also note other simple materials specific to the suggested activities.

SAMPLE SESSION 1
First Impressions in the Maze

AT A GLANCE

Goal: Girls explore relationship obstacles and the impact first impressions have on relationships.

- What's in Your Maze?
- Choices for the Journey
- Beneath the Surface
- Closing Ceremony: Going for Goals

MATERIALS

- Paper and markers, including a thin, permanent marker
- Envelopes
- Posterboard, newsprint, or any large paper
- Inflatable beach ball or other inexpensive ball marked with "Beneath the Surface" questions (see list at right and page 20 of girls' book)

ADVANCE PREP

Inflate the beach ball, if necessary, and use a thin permanent marker to write "Beneath the Surface" questions from the list below around the ball. Then use masking tape to cover the questions. The tape gets peeled off as girls pass the ball and answer a question beneath. (This is a perfect opportunity for girl volunteers to assist.)

Sample "Beneath the Surface" Questions

Sample questions are also on page 20 of the girls' book. Mix in some of the ones below, or any of your own, to give the Cadettes something new to think about.

- Something obvious about me is . . .

- Only a few other people know that I . . .

- My biggest fear is . . .

- A time when my impression of someone was very wrong was . . .

- The nicest thing someone has ever done for me is . . .

- Two words people use to describe me are . . .

- Before people get to know me, they assume I . . .

- The funniest thing that ever happened to me was . . .

- A song that always makes me happy is . . .

- If I could have only one artistic talent, it would be . . .

- If I could excel at only one sport it would be . . .

- My family made me proud when . . .

- The first thing I notice about someone new is . . .

- The first thing I hope others notice about me when we meet is . . .

- Three qualities a leader should have are . . .

NO BALL, NO TIME?

Write each question on a scrap of paper and place all the scraps in a bag. Instead of throwing a ball, girls can pass the bag and pick a slip.

What's In Your Maze?

This activity gets girls thinking together about the relationship issues that make their lives "mazelike." It also engages girls in getting to know one another and beginning to team up.

Start by asking the Cadettes to form small groups of two to four girls. (In large groups or groups where girls don't know each other, count off the groups so that girls have a chance to meet and can bypass any discomfort involved in choosing teams.)

Invite girls to introduce themselves in their small groups—perhaps saying something about themselves, such as their favorite thing to do when they have free time. But encourage the girls to vary their answers, so that those girls who know others might share something new.

Give each group a piece of paper or cardboard (or anything they can write on) and markers or pens and ask them to take a few minutes to draw a maze of their own—complex or simple.

Then ask each group to brainstorm the ways in which their lives are like a maze, using real-life experiences. You might say, or even post, some thought starters for girls, such as:

• Who sits where at lunch time?

• Whom do you count on? Where do you "meet them" in the maze?

• Ever have a conflict with best friends? Does that shift your path?

• Ouch! Something hurt your feelings. What?

• Where do new friends come in?

• Do bullies affect you? Maybe you sometimes are the bullies?

• What do you talk about online?

• Who said what to whom?

• What will be going on for you over the next few years? What new things might get added to your maze?

• Who are the adults who help you through the maze?

• How about friends? What do they do that helps?

Invite the teams to mark their mazes with sketches, text bubbles, or doodles that show the relationship issues they navigate in their lives. Encourage them to show both the challenges that occur in the maze and the "resources" they use to overcome those challenges (such as support from others they trust). Perhaps they also want to show the role of great friendships in the maze and other "positives" that occur in their interactions.

As the teams finish up, ask them to think of one phrase or slogan (something short that could fit on a bumper sticker) that completes the sentence:

Our lives are like a maze because . . .

Call the full group back together and invite each team to present its maze—and some of the issues they illustrated on it. In groups where the girls do not know one another, the members of each mini team might also introduce themselves to the larger group before sharing their maze. Ask each team to end its presentation by sharing its "bumper sticker" slogan.

Put the heading "Our life is a maze because" on a poster board (or any paper you have handy). As each team gives its "bumper sticker" phrase, add it to the board (or ask a girl to), forming a team poem as you go. Let girls know that their mini mazes and the team poem they just created represent a giant maze that you are all entering together.

Transition to a discussion about the purpose of the journey. Perhaps use some discussion starters like these (but feel free to reword them in your own voice):

- We've been looking at how our lives are like mazes. Mazes have twists, turns, and unexpected changes—just like the relationships we navigate in our lives.

- And even though most mazes have just one true path, navigating life doesn't have to be a one-size-fits-all solution. You can confront obstacles, try shortcuts, and take chances as you try to find the right way.

- Along the passageways of this aMAZE journey, we'll explore how to have the best and the healthiest relationships we can—and how to be really confident about how we navigate them.

- We'll also think about—and experience—how, when we bring more confidence and skill to our relationships, we can create better relationships that may actually improve the world around us.

Refer girls to the aMAZE map on the cover of their books. Talk about how it gives them the chance to see some of the topics they will explore along the journey, and how the passageways connect.

TIPS FOR SHARING AND DISCUSSING

When inviting girls to share ideas and feelings, always let them know that it's OK to "pass" or just offer a brief thought or two. And let girls know that it's fine to share general ideas without getting into specifics. For example, they might say, "True friendships are a great resource to get out of a tangle in the maze" rather than, "My friends ____ and ____ are so great because they ____ ." Repeat these instructions as needed throughout the journey, depending on the comfort level of sharing that the girls show.

GET CREATIVE

If the group has time (today or another day) and the interest, encourage the girls to create "life is a maze" poems, drawings, or song lyrics. They might do this on their own or in small teams—and they can build from their "Life is a maze because . . . " team poem. They might even want to display their creations for themselves or others. They could be a part of an awareness project or workshop for younger girls that they integrate into their Take Action plans as the journey progresses.

Choices for the Journey

Invite the girls to form one big circle. Mention that circles are an important way to relate; everyone can see one another, so everyone is equal and can focus their energy together as a team. Then, suggest that the team now create a plan for how this journey through aMAZE will unfold. If there are any time limits to work around, mention them up front, so girls know the parameters within which they can get creative. And if the team has plenty of time, encourage the girls to stretch out the trip.

Perhaps a few of the girls would like to capture what the group discusses (just the big points) on a large sheet of paper that the team can refer back to along the journey.

Introduce each area of choice-making, and invite girls to participate in creating a great experience. Here are some of the choices to discuss and some ideas about how to approach them:

Awards

Find out if the girls are interested in earning the Interact, Diplomat, and Peacemaker awards during the journey. (They can earn one, two, or all three.) Review the steps to the awards as given on page 9 of the girls' book.

- Mention that the Take Action Project can be a team effort in which girls will use their leadership skills to contribute to building positive relationships in a community of their choice.

- If girls are not interested in the Diplomat Award, which involves doing a Take Action Project, what would they like to do instead during Sessions 5-7? Are there any topics in their book that they want to talk more about during this time? Do the girls want to plan these sessions themselves?

Using Ceremonies to Connect at Each Meeting

Explain that ceremonies, even short ones, can be a great way to take a little time out together to mark each Cadette gathering as special and separate from the rest of the day. Ceremonies can be a fun way for girls to connect and relate to each other. Ask the girls if they have any ideas for ceremonies, such as lighting candles or listening to music—or offer up some of the suggestions on the next page. Then ask the girls if they want to have ceremonies to open and/or close their time together. Find out which girls might like to plan and lead some ceremonies—perhaps even circulate a sign-up list.

Sample Ceremonies

- **Create a "conversation starters" jar** in which girls place slips of paper on which they've written words or phrases that capture various relationship topics (such as cliques, peer pressure, being yourself) and the leadership qualities or skills that go along with them. Each week, one girl chooses a slip of paper and then starts a short group talk about what's written on it.

- **The girls take turns selecting songs** that reflect relationship issues they are experiencing or might encounter along the maze of life. At the start of each session, ask a girl to volunteer to play her song for the group (even if just from a cell phone), and then take a few minutes to relate the song to aMAZE.

- **Each girl brings pictures from magazines** that reflect a direction or an interest she hopes to follow in life's maze. Create a team poster from those pictures. For an opening ceremony, encourage girls to talk about what their pictures mean to them and the leadership skills needed to navigate life's maze successfully in that way. If space allows, leave the team poster hanging throughout each session.

NO CEREMONIES? NO WORRIES

If ceremonies don't interest the girls, don't be concerned. Upcoming sessions offer suggestions for simple ceremonies (no planning needed) that the Cadettes can perform spontaneously, should they decide they want an opening of some kind.

Team Agreement

Close the discussion by inviting girls to make a team agreement.

Say something like: *As we travel through aMAZE, it's important that we trust one another. What do we need to promise each other, so that we can have a really positive experience relating to others along this journey?* Then, offer these ideas:

- *We will watch our body language when we talk and listen (no eye rolling!)*

- *If we have a conflict with someone in the group, we can . . .*

- *If we have a different opinion, we can . . .*

- *Gossip would be hurtful because . . .*

Perhaps one of the girls can capture the team agreement on paper so it can be brought to all meetings and the girls can check in on how they are doing.

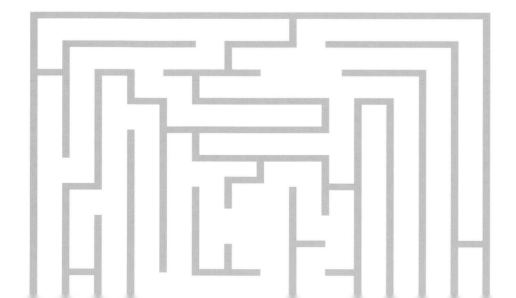

LARGE GROUP?

If your Cadette group has more than 10-12 girls, perhaps divide them into smaller groups—each with its own ball. That way, every girl can have a chance to answer a question.

Beneath the Surface

This team activity, featured on page 20 of the girls' book, lets the Cadettes discover their similarities and reveal their differences. It also gets them thinking about how first impressions and assumptions might hinder their relationships.

Have girls stand in a circle. Explain:

- *When the ball is passed to you, remove one piece of tape and answer the question underneath.*

- *After answering, toss the ball to a girl who has not yet had a turn.*

Then give the ball to one of the girls to start the process. After each girl has had a chance to catch the ball and respond to a question, start a conversation about first impressions. Guide a meaningful discussion by perhaps asking some of these questions:

- *Have you ever thought you knew something about someone else but found out you were wrong? Explain.*

- *How do first impressions impact teams?*

- *What happens when we act as if everyone is exactly the way we first perceived them? Talk about how this can include or exclude others.*

- *When you walk into a room and realize you don't know anyone else there, what do you usually do to feel comfortable with others?*

- *What do you base your first impression on?*

- *How accurate do you think your first impressions are when meeting people for the first time?*

- *When have you had a completely wrong first impression of someone, and what changed your mind?*

- *Can you think of situations when people had a wrong first impression of you? What did you do to give an accurate impression of yourself?*

- *What could you do so that first impressions allow you to see people for who they really are, rather than who you think they are?*

Closing Ceremony: Going for Goals

Ask the girls to form small teams of three to four so they will be able to talk easily with one another and gain support for the personal goals they are going to identify. (There tends to be greater personal commitment when sharing a goal in a small group, as opposed to a large one.)

Give a piece of paper to each girl and explain the activity by saying something like:

- *Today we've been exploring how, when solving a maze, you rely on certain strategies or techniques. The same is true when you're striving toward a goal in life. Your goal is much like the end point you're trying to reach when you navigate a maze.*

Then:

- Ask the girls to brainstorm the relationship issues that most affect them, whether it's standing up to a bully, getting out of a negative clique, improving a friendship, making more friends, or something else entirely.

- Each girl then chooses which issue (or two) she wants to solve for herself, and writes it (or them) on her sheet of paper. She then puts the paper in an envelope that she addresses to herself.

- Collect the sealed envelopes and let girls know you'll return them at the end of the journey, so they can reflect on how they progressed toward their goal. Let them know the reflection will be just for them—unless they choose to share.

FOR THE NEXT SESSION

Ask girls to bring to the next session a small, empty box or other container and some odds and ends for decorating it (wrapping paper, ribbon, beads, glue). Encourage them to bring items to share, too. If everyone brings a little something different, the decorating will be that much more interesting.

Ask if any girls want to volunteer to:

- Plan a simple opening ceremony.

- Lead a brainstorm about friendship qualities (pages 31–32 in the girls' book)

- Host an "Ask the Expert Talk Show" (page 45 in this guide)

"Some people come into our lives and quickly go.
Some people stay a while, leave footprints
in our hearts, and we are never, ever the same."

—Flavia Weedn

YELLING   secrets

Gossip   Rumors

hitting/   exclusion   Rumors
kicking

MANIPULATION   silent treatment

Hierarchy

Clique   LIES
LIES
LIES

SAMPLE SESSION 2
Navigating Friendships

AT A GLANCE

Goal: Girls understand how stereotypes impact relationships and identify the personal qualities they seek in, and bring to, healthy friendships.

- Opening Ceremony
- Peacemaker Kits
- How Do You Know?
- Stereotypes and You
- Circle of Friends
- Talk Show: Ask the Expert
- For Peacemaker Kits

MATERIALS

- An assortment of small empty containers (tins from mints, jewelry-size boxes, even small take-out food containers) for those girls who might not bring their own
- Odds and ends for decorating the containers (beads, buttons, stickers, wrapping paper) and glue
- Paper (two sheets for each girl) and pens

ADVANCE PREP

Peacemaker Kits

At the start of this session, girls will create their Peacemaker Kits, which they will use to collect tips and tools they can use to create peace—one interaction at a time—in their lives and in the world around them. The kits also serve as a special memory of the journey. Think of them as scrapbooks in which each girl saves the ideas she finds most meaningful as she winds her way through the passageways of aMAZE.

Advance Prep by Cadettes

If you have girl volunteers for this session, they might want to:

- Lead the Circle of Friends activity and discussion (page 44)

- Prepare and play a role in "Ask the Expert" (page 45)

TIPS FOR TALKING ABOUT . . .

FRIENDSHIPS

It often seems that girls are supposed to know what it means to be a good friend, but nobody ever really talks to them about how to be a good friend. In this session, it's important to create an environment in which girls feel they can really open up about what they need from their friends, what they bring to their friendships, and how to make and keep true friends. As they get to know each other and spend time together as a team, invite them to revisit their team agreement (written in Session 1) and talk together about how they are doing—and what they need to add or improve.

STEREOTYPES

The girls' book (page 22) offers a definition of stereotypes—generalizations or assumptions that we form about people who are "members" of a particular group—and explains how they are longer-lasting, and therefore perhaps more harmful, than first impressions.

Talking about stereotypes with the girls can cause some confusion, so you'll find it useful to encourage them to focus on specific examples of stereotyping that have affected them or examples they can identify from the media. Explain to the girls that by making guesses or assumptions about stereotypes they are unfamiliar with, we may actually end up perpetuating those stereotypes.

If you are comfortable doing so, share an experience you have had when a stereotype hurt you, or when you let a stereotype influence how you treated someone. Share what you learned as a result and how you have since tried to adjust your thinking. Your honesty may make the girls more comfortable in sharing their experiences—and more secure in knowing how to overcome stereotypes.

Opening Ceremony

Invite girls to do a short opening ceremony as discussed at the first gathering. This is a chance to connect and clear their heads. If they want a little something but have nothing prepared, suggest they: go around in a circle and say one thing they do that they think makes them a great friend. Or, ask one girl to choose a quote that pops out at her from the girls' book and then each girl can say a few thoughts about what the quote means to her. If no one really wants a ceremony, get going with the next activity.

Peacemaker Kits

Girls might like some music on while they do this! You can even have some "starter supplies" out, so they can jump in as soon as they arrive. If you have time restraints, you can keep "the making" to 10–15 minutes. Girls can finish up on their own, or while some of the next discussions are taking place. But if girls are into crafts, talk to them about building time into a future gathering for this interest. What would they like to make? Any "souvenirs" for the journey?

How Do You Know?

This exercise continues the topic begun at the first session (with the "What Lies Beneath" exercise), going deeper by asking girls to explore how stereotypes negatively influence first impressions and relationships.

Begin with a short discussion about what a stereotype is. You could, for example, ask a few questions like:

- *What does it mean to "stereotype" other people?*

- *How do stereotypes influence who we choose to interact with and how we interact with them?*

Depending on the girls' responses, you can offer a few basic points about stereotyping (based on what they have on page 22 of their book) to make sure all girls are thinking and talking from a similar starting point.

Continue the discussion by inviting girls to identify examples of stereotypes that are used in portraying a character on a TV show they enjoy. (Or they might think of a movie or cartoon or even a music video.)

Ask girls to talk about who is hurt by the stereotype. Do they think it is wrong for the show to use it?

Wrap up this part of the discussion by reminding girls that their conversation relates to one of the Interact Challenges they can choose to earn the Interact Award (see page 12–15 of the girls' book). Are they interested in taking this challenge? Do any of the examples from their conversation trouble them enough to boycott the show for a week or two—or forever? Would they mention it to other friends, too?

Stereotypes and You

Invite the girls to do the "Break Down Those Stereotypes!" activity on page 23 of their books, on their own or in pairs. This engages girls directly in thinking about stereotypes that are hurtful to them.

Then ask the girls to move around (as pairs or individuals) and trade their stories of how a stereotype had impacted them. (If the group is small, you could do this as one team discussion.)

After the girls have had a chance to share their perspectives on stereotypes, start a team discussion about any insights they have gained. Conversation prompts could include:

• *How does it feel to hear about how stereotypes have hurt you?*

• *How do these stereotypes get carried forward and passed on?*

• *What are some examples of things you might change and ask other people to change to stop some of the stereotyping you have heard about from each other?*

• *Have you ever closed the door on a friendship because of stereotypes? What could you do instead, next time?*

dresses So friendly
funny
big smile ears stick out
talks too much
waaay popular
SUPER Too much eyeliner
JOCK LOUD AND PUSHY

Circle of Friends

In this activity and discussion, which relates to the friendship activities that begin on page 31 of the girls' book, the Cadettes can recognize the characteristics they look for in a friend, and identify the qualities they bring to a friendship.

Pass out paper and markers and then:

- Ask: *What are the qualities you look for in your friends?* Create a list of qualities and also look at some of the qualities listed on page 32 of your books.

- Ask girls to draw a circle. Explain that the circle represents their circle of friends.

- Ask girls to write the words in the middle of their circle that describe the qualities they look for in friends.

- Next, around the outside of the circle, ask them to write words that they feel describe the qualities they bring to friendships. After doing so, have them draw an even bigger circle (or different shape) around the outside to encompass all the qualities.

When the girls have finished their circles, invite them to share what they wrote. If your group is large, keep the sharing process intimate by having girls share in smaller groups (five to eight girls) instead of sharing with the group as a whole.

Now wrap up the discussion, or invite a girl volunteer to wrap it up, by asking some questions such as these:

- *Are there any words missing from our lists? What might we want to add?*

- *Are there words on the list that describe friendships but also sound negative? Explain.*

- *Are there qualities you feel you bring to your friendships that your friends don't reciprocate or vice versa?*

- *How can you be the kind of friend that you want to have?*

- *Why are healthy friendships so important to us?*

- *Do we always make choices based on these positive qualities or do other things sometimes influence us (clothes, money, who someone's friends are)? Why?*

MORE FRIENDSHIP, PLEASE

Depending on the time and interest of the group, you might also explore two other activities in the girls' book: "My Kind of Friend: What Really Matters" on page 31, where girls rank how they choose friends, and the "Top 10 Great Friendship Tips" on page 33.

Talk Show: Ask the Expert

This activity puts girls in the lead as they provide advice to one another about making and keeping true friendships. Encourage a playful spirit—but not one that pokes fun at any individuals.

- Get girls moving around, asking them to form teams of three. Pass out scrap paper and pens.

- Explain that girls will take turns playing the host of the talk show "Ask the Expert." Say something like: This week's topic is about friendship, and we have several guests who have friendship dilemmas.

- Ask girls to volunteer as guests (who have a friendship issue they want advice on) and hosts (who give the advice).

- Share the sample scenarios provided on the next page to get the girls started, and then invite girls to make up their own.

- Each guest gets a turn being "onstage" with a host to present her dilemma. The host can ask for audience assistance to get the best solutions to each question.

After the "Ask the Expert" show, bring the group back together (and a little more on the serious side!) and start a discussion, using questions such as these to guide the conversation:

- *How realistic is the advice each guest was offered? Would you follow this advice?*

- *In your life, who can you count on to give good advice about friendship issues?*

- *In what ways do people rely on leaders to serve as advice columnists when certain decisions or choices need to be made?*

- *Any skills or tips learned to add to your Peacemaker Kits?*

SAFE SPACE CHECK-IN

Now is a good point to stop briefly and check in to see that girls are feeling safe in the group, and are comfortable talking and sharing with one another. Talking about relationships can be tough! Invite the team to check in on how they are doing on their team agreement. See if they might want to add anything. Examples might include:

This conversation is confidential; it stays just among us.

Let's remember that we all care about one another.

Let's not allow blaming.

SAMPLE SCENARIOS FOR TALK SHOW

GUEST 1

My best friend, Alicia, just moved away, and I'm so lonely! I know I need to make new friends, but I just don't know how—Alicia and I have been friends forever! I'm not sure I can explain what I want in a friend. How do I choose a friend? What's important to look for in a friendship? I know it feels good to have friends, but what's the reason why it's good to have friends? Can you help?

_____

_____

_____

_____

GUEST 2

I like joking around with this girl named Kerry, who sits next to me in science. I have been thinking of asking her to study or maybe go shopping with me. But how can I know if Kerry will be interested in being more than just an "in-school" friend?

_____

_____

_____

_____

GUEST 3

I'm so confused! I can't figure out who my BFF is. Some days, I like Gayle the best, because I know that I can be serious with her when I have a problem and she'll always listen. But other days, I prefer Isabel, because she makes me laugh harder than anyone I've ever known. How can I know who my BFF really is?

_____

_____

_____

_____

For Peacemaker Kits

Give out small scraps of paper and ask the girls to jot down skills or tips they thought about today that they can use in their lives and pass on to others. You might remind them about the topics covered: first impressions, stereotypes, choosing friends, and qualities we seek and bring to friendships. What one or two specific ideas will girls take away? The girls can put these in their Peacemaker Kits.

Optional Activity: "Masking" Feelings

In this activity, the girls compare their "outer" selves with their "inner" selves while enjoying some arts and crafts.

- Each girl cuts out an oversized face shape from poster board (with cut-out eyes and mouth if they like).

- Girls then decorate the mask. One side—the outside—represents what they feel people see/know/believe about them. The other side represents what each girl feels about herself (things going on inside her that others don't necessarily know or see).

- When they are finished decorating, ask the girls to share with the group what each side of their mask represents—if they're comfortable doing so.

FOR THE NEXT SESSION

Before girls head out:

Ask for volunteers who want to have a lead role in the next session. You might huddle with them for a minute now or talk to them between sessions, maybe even electronically.

Congratulate girls for the thoughtful work they are doing on relationship skills.

Remind those who are interested about the "Interact Challenges." Review some of the challenges, such as creating special messages for friends or mending an old friendship, as listed in the chart on page 12–13 of the girls' book.

EXTRAS

FRIENDSHIP PICKUP LINES

Create a Top 10 list by brainstorming together: What questions can be used to initiate a conversation with a potential new friend? Offer some examples, such as:

- Would you like to be my lab partner?

- Cute! Where did you get it?

CELEB PALS

Ask girls if they would want to be friends with a particular celebrity they know of. Why or why not? Offer up celebrities such as America Ferrera, Blake Lively, and Raven Simone. Let the girls discuss the kind of friends they think celebrities like these would make. Ask: What do you base friendship on?

SAMPLE SESSION 3
Cliques and Conflicts

AT A GLANCE

Goal: Girls identify various types of peer pressure, practice strategies for managing peer pressure, explore the damaging clique behaviors, and practice important conflict resolution tools.

- Opening Ceremony
- Friendship Game
- Where Do You Stand?

- Cliquish?
- "I-Statements"

ADVANCE PREP

Girl Volunteers

If any girls have signed on for active roles this session, you might talk with them about:

- An opening ceremony of their choice

- A fun team game (two options are given but girls might have more ideas)

- Scenarios they suggest for "Where Do You Stand"

TIPS FOR TALKING ABOUT . . .

PEER PRESSURE

By middle school, girls have probably heard the words "peer pressure" used often—and might find it a little "eye-rolling." The "Where Do You Stand?" activity on page 42 of their book asks them to think about pressure in a new way—by using the lens of their values to make decisions.

An environment where honest, open, and kind dialogue and confidentiality is respected will encourage the girls to be engaged. Talk of boys or jealousy may get uncomfortable for the girls, but it gives you the chance to explain that these issues arise all the time, and that the best way to work through them is with people you trust.

CLIQUES

You'll be guiding girls to explore the exclusive and hurtful dynamics that can happen in cliques. For this purpose, think of a clique as an informal and restricted social group formed by people who share common interests or patterns of behavior.

In this case, "exclusive" refers to behaviors that keep other people out. The opposite is "inclusive" behavior—it welcomes people in.

"I-STATEMENTS"

In relationships, girls need to assert their feelings and needs. The "I-Statements" activity provides them with a "formula," and the vocabulary and confidence to let others know what they need in relationships. "I-Statements" are also an important tool for resolving conflict. (They work wonders in adult relationships, too! You might want to take a minute and brush up on the "formula" on page 55 before the session.)

Cliques and Conflicts

Opening Ceremony

Invite the girls to reconnect with one another using a ceremony of their choice—or jump into a friendship game.

Friendship Games

Girls can vote on one of these physical, active games or choose one they already know and love. After the game, take a few minutes to talk about what it feels like to belong in a group where you can get a little silly without worrying what other people think.

Back-to-Back

This activity requires girls to get moving, so if they have energy to spare, this might be particularly good for them.

- Girls break into pairs, looking for partners of similar size if possible.

- The pairs of girls lock arms with their backs to each other.

- Each pair slowly lowers to the floor, kicks their legs out straight, and then raises up again.

- Once each set of partners is standing up, pairs of girls should become quartets (two pairs join together), and the sequence is repeated (lock, lower, kick, raise up).

- Quartets can join with other quartets, then octets join with octets, repeating the sequence until the entire group has locked arms and is lowering and rising together.

Shoe Factory

By the time girls finish this activity, they'll probably have a Twister-like configuration going. It starts with the whole group of girls standing in a large circle, shoulder to shoulder.

Everyone removes their shoes and puts them in the center of the circle.

Once the pile of shoes is made, each girl chooses two different shoes other than her own and puts them on (only halfway if they're too small).

Each girl needs to find the mate to her shoes and put her foot up against it. By the time the final pair is matched, the group will probably be a tangled mess of legs, causing lots of laughter.

Where Do You Stand?

This activity gives girls a chance to take a stance on peer pressure, clarifying their own values in the process. Start by inviting girls to think about times when they have been pressured or perhaps pressured others to do things that go against their values. You can use some of these points to begin:

- *We all have experiences that test our values. Do we ever trade in what we believe just so we can belong? How do we feel after doing that?*

- *We also have times that we pressure others. Why? Can that sometimes be "for their own good?" (Pressure can sometimes be for good. Can you give examples?)*

- *Sometimes the pressure to do something you don't want to do can be silent. Can you think of examples of silent pressure?*

- *Have you ever accomplished something you didn't think you'd be able to do, but were able to because of someone else's influence?*

Transition from the discussion by saying something like:

We are going to do an activity to push one another to explore what it feels like to stand up for our values. We really have to trust one another and uphold our team agreement for this to be meaningful. Ready?

Then, with masking tape, mark a line down the center of the room. On one end, put a piece of paper on the floor with the number 10. On the other end, put a 1. In the middle, mark a 5.

Tell the girls that you (or girl volunteers) are going to read aloud a scenario and if they think it's OK, they go to number 10. If they feel it's not OK, they go to number 1. If they're "on the fence," they go to number 5.

After each scenario is read and each girl takes her stance on the line, invite each to talk about why she stood where she did. Do any girls want to try to persuade others to stand somewhere else? Why or why not? When the girls have exhausted what they have to say, read another scenario. Some scenarios may invite more conversation than others, and you may work through a handful fairly quickly as girls become more engaged.

You might prompt the girls' conversation by asking:

What are you really saying if you go to the middle, on number 5? Are you worried about taking a stand? What are your worries? Trying to please everyone? What would help you make a decision?

If you are standing near "1," do you think there are things people could say or do that would make you inch your way down the line? What? How would you answer?

If you are standing near "10," do you think there are times someone could persuade you down the line? How?

Scenarios

There are more scenarios here than you'll need. Use those most appropriate for your group of Cadettes. If other issues have come up among the girls, add them. Or, pause for a few minutes and invite the girls to offer up some of their own—after doing some of these:

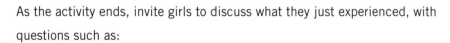

It's good to tell a friend she should study harder and try to get better grades.

If your friend really wants you to attend her piano recital because she needs a confidence boost, you should go—even though it sounds like a lot of clanging to you.

It's OK to attend a party at your best friend's house even if her parents aren't there the entire night.

Smoking with some friends isn't a problem, since it's not something you do all the time.

I'd cancel plans with my friend if my crush asked me out at the last minute.

If you're jealous of someone, it's OK to be mean to her, as long as you aren't physically violent.

If a friend is really hurting herself through behavior that you find scary, you should keep it a secret, no matter what.

You can watch a movie at a friend's house (or elsewhere) that your parents would never let you watch at home.

It's OK to tell your parents the party is "girls-only," even though there will be boys and you hope to meet up with a special one there.

Sometimes you have to skip the fun to get some homework done.

You can say crazy, risky, untrue things about yourself online. It doesn't really matter.

Sometimes you just have to stop hanging out with some girls because others don't think they're cool.

It's cool to disrespect your parents in front of friends.

It's good for your image to drink some alcohol at parties even though you don't want to.

You need to try out for a team sport or cheerleading, because everyone does.

It's important to act like you have more money than you really have.

Sometimes it's OK to make critical comments or put others down in the presence of certain friends.

As the activity ends, invite girls to discuss what they just experienced, with questions such as:

- *Which scenarios really made an impression on you? Explain.*

- *How does this activity help you think about the effects of peer pressure and how you use your values to make decisions?*

- *How do you want others to view your response to peer pressure?*

- *Does standing up for a value make you feel like a leader? Why or why not?*

Cliquish?

In this activity and discussion, the girls determine whether they and their friends tend to be cliquish (exclude or pressure others) or inclusive (welcoming others and accepting differences). Transition from the discussion of the scenarios by saying something like: Sometimes when we are feeling pressured to do something we really don't want to, it might be related to being in a clique. Can anyone think of an example?

Next, invite girls to brainstorm two lists: "Clique" and "Circle of Belonging." (Ask for a girl to volunteer to play scribe and capture the lists on newsprint or other paper.)

Start with Clique and invite girls to shout out words, phrases, songs, movies, or feelings related to clique behavior. For example, girls might say: "left out" or "you don't belong" or "wannabee" or "popular."

Then, ask the girls to brainstorm words, phrases, or feelings that come to mind when they think about an inclusive circle of belonging.

Once the lists are created, invite the girls to discuss them—perhaps a girl can even lead the discussion. To guide the conversation, use a few prompts, such as:

- *Based on the lists you just made, are there times when you and some of your friends act like a clique?*

- *What experiences have you had that feel more like what we described on our "circle of belonging list?" How could you create more of that?*

- *What could you change (if anything) about how you and your friends interact with others?*

- *How do cliques get started?*

- *What do girls get from cliques?*

- *How can cliques hurt those not in them?*

Wrap up by inviting the girls to check out pages 56–57 of their book for suggestions on how to assess the groups they belong to. An interesting question to discuss together is: Are there any ways in which this Girl Scout Cadette group is a clique? If the answer is "yes," what might girls do to change that? If "no," what do girls like about the group dynamics that they could try to create in other groups they belong to?

TOSS IT!

Sometimes brainstorms "pop along" with more energy when the participants toss around a ball (or stuffed animal "mascot" or anything that won't hurt!) while talking.

"I-Statements": The Key to Resolving Conflicts

Now engage the girls in thinking about how throughout life, conflicts are a potential relationship obstacle. Invite them to check out the suggestions for resolving conflicts on page 63 of their book. Start a discussion with questions such as:

- *Does anyone have an example of a time when you decided to let a conflict go? How did that feel?*

- *Have you ever tried talking through a conflict only to have your effort backfire?*

- *Have you ever shifted your point of view on a conflict—really looked at it from the other person's point of view?*

Then say something like: *Choosing to resolve a conflict usually means we have to talk it through. Let's look at how "I-Statements" can be a powerful tool for describing how you are feeling and what you need when you have a conflict in a relationship.*

Engage the girls in using "I-Statements" with the following exercise. Begin by saying something like:

- *We've all had experiences where our feelings were hurt. Perhaps you had a strong opinion about something and blurted out some words in an angry way that didn't solve the problem but worsened it. Or maybe you kept your real feelings bottled up, just waiting to explode.*

- *We're now going to practice using "I-Statements," which let you feel confident communicating difficult feelings with sensitivity and respect. You can speak up—in a way that's powerful and respectful—instead of keeping your feelings bottled up or communicating in an attacking, blaming way.*

Refer the girls to page 63 in their book and talk through what "I-Statements" are. You might want to post the general formula on a large sheet of paper so everyone can keep it in mind:

> When you _____ (describe a specific action that hurts you)
>
> I feel _____ (say your feeling)
>
> because _____ (why the action connects to your feeling)

A good "I-Statement" focuses on a specific behavior and how it affects you. Here's an example: When you make fun of the way I dress, I feel discouraged because your opinion is important to me. A not-so-good example is: When you act like a jerk, I feel hurt. Ask the girls:

- *Can you hear the difference?*

- *In the first example, there is a specific example of one behavior that causes hurt feelings.*

- *In the second example, there is no specific example, and the person the comment is aimed at will probably feel attacked and get defensive, making the conflict worse.*

Ask girls for examples of "feeling" words they can use in "I-Statements" and encourage them to check out the examples on pages 66–67 of their book (also listed at right).

Break girls into pairs, and invite them to look at the scenarios on pages 66–67 of their book. Ask them to practice responding with their own "I-Statements." You might need to coach them a bit so they get the hang of it.

Notice that you have examples of "I-Statements" for the five scenarios that girls will be trying on the next page. These are just examples—you and the girls might have other ideas. The goal is for the Cadettes to become confident about identifying a specific behavior they want to address, and at ease using an "I-Statement" and a description of their feelings in their conversation.

You can also ask the girls to think of "I-Statements" that might help them respond to a conflict they recently experienced.

When the girls are finished, ask the group as a whole to share their thoughts on:

- How "I-Statements" are different from other ways of responding

- How being assertive with "I-Statements" made them feel

- Whether they think they can implement this type of communication in their own lives

"I-Statements" Examples

Over the past month, your best friend has been distant. You know she's busy with school and her part-time job, but every time you chat with her, she talks about her problems and then rushes you off the phone when you begin to talk about your day.	*You are so selfish. You are not the only one who's busy and who has a lot going on! You know I have a dance competition coming up and have been practicing three hours a day with my group to get the routines right!*	*When you rush me off the phone when I have problems, I feel hurt and unsupported. When can you make time for me?*
You have a morning class with one friend and then meet up with everyone in your group for lunch. Lately, when you and your friend are together in class, she always agrees with what you say. But when you're in your full group, she says things to put you down. The rest of the group is oblivious since they're not with you in the morning.	*Why are you being so two-faced?! You're not impressing anyone by being a hypocrite!*	*When you publicly criticized me at lunch, I felt confused about our friendship. You agree with me on almost everything when we're hanging out alone. Can we talk about this?*
Nearly every day your friend mentions how expensive her outfit is and how her mom keeps buying her new clothes for the season. Your parents think it's silly to spend so much on clothes you'll grow out of in a year. You do, too, but you're still dying for some new designer jeans.	*Why do you constantly brag about your clothes? You are not better or smarter just because you wear cool designer clothes every day!*	*When you talk about how expensive your clothes are, I feel put down because I only have nondesigner clothes.*
You hear your best friend ask your boyfriend to help her with her homework on Friday afternoon, although you and he have a standing date every week to do just that.	*I can't believe you would ask my boyfriend to help you with homework! You know he helps me with homework on Friday afternoons. Are you trying to steal him from me?*	*Solve It Yourself!* *When you _____ I feel _____!* **Example for coaching girls:** *When I found out you asked my boyfriend to help you with your homework, I felt betrayed. Next time, can you mention it to me first?*
Your soccer buddy teases you in front of the team about missing a goal. When you try to defend yourself, she calls you a "wuss" for not being able to take a joke.	*You are always mean to me. You are such a horrible friend!*	*Solve It Yourself!* *When you _____ I feel _____!* **Example for coaching girls:** *When you call me names, like "wuss," I feel embarrassed.*

For Peacemaker Kits

Invite girls to take some time to add new ideas and tools to their Peacemaker Kits. You might remind them about today's passageways through the maze, which involved:

• Clarifying and using values to deal with peer pressure

• Assessing and changing clique behavior

• Techniques for resolving conflict

• Using "I-Statements"

Encourage girls to think not just about how these strategies could improve their own friendships but how they might increase peace in general if people around the world used them.

BEFORE LEAVING AMAZE FOR THE DAY . . .

Ask if any girls want to volunteer to take a lead in the next session. And encourage the Cadettes to check out the Interact Challenges related to cliques, gossip, and "I-Statements." Perhaps they want to pursue some of these challenges as a path toward the Interact Award.

"We must reject the view that, to be a victor, you must have a victim; to stand tall, you must stand on someone."

— Harriet Woods, U.S. politician, journalist, and civic leader (1927-2007)

SAMPLE SESSION 4
Caution: Bullies Straight Ahead

AT A GLANCE

Goal: Girls identify and address bullying behavior and gain greater understanding of their roles as witnesses. They also develop strategies for building safe online relationships.

- Opening Ceremony
- Interact Challenge Check-In
- Definitions, Please
- Take Back the Power

- Flip the Script
- Surfing Through Cyberspace
- The Girl Scout Law Meets the Virtual World
- Toward Peace

ADVANCE PREP

About Bullying Behavior

Bullying often occurs through relational aggression: rumors, secrets, lies, betrayal, gossip, taunting, exclusion, harassment, silent treatment, and behind-the-back actions that can damage relationships and leave scars.

This passageway of aMAZE offers girls ways to identify relational aggression and other types of bullying, and stop them. It will be important for you to encourage honesty and an atmosphere of respect, especially if someone admits she tends to exhibit bullying behavior (and others agree). Also, depending on the term that's most familiar to your group and/or their maturity, feel free to use "bullying" and "relational aggression" interchangeably when referring to actions that are geared toward the destruction of a person's relationships with others.

PLEASE NOTE

For this session, the terms "cyber" and "virtual" refer to anything girls do in cyberspace— e-mail, text messaging, surfing the Web, or any other activities where primary communication is conducted through technology rather than face-to-face and in real time or using truly archival methods, such as hand-written letters or telephone voice mails.

PLEASE NOTE

Whenever possible, use the term "bullying behavior" rather than "bully," so the emphasis is on a girl's actions—not her whole person.

If the girls have let you know that emotional or physical violence is an issue for them, you will want to identify an expert in your community to help out. Your Girl Scout council or the girls' schools are good places to start.

CYBER RELATIONSHIPS

The online world often seems to change overnight. If you don't know much about the kinds of "cyber issues" girls face or just want to brush up on what's new in teen virtual talk and cyber safety, check out these sites:

netsmartz.org

stopbullyingnow.hrsa.gov

Opening Ceremony

Welcome the girls and invite them to do an opening ceremony of their choice.

Interact Challenge Check-In

Ask if any of the girls have been doing Interact Challenges and want to talk about them. Have girls tried to "pass it forward" by inviting others to follow their action? Do any girls have results to share?

Definitions, Please

Let the girls know that the obstacle in today's aMAZE passageway is bullying behavior. Invite them to define what bullying means and then provide this information to clarify their thinking:

> The Anti-Bullying Alliance, a UK-based network of organizations that works to reduce bullying and create safe environments for youth, defines bullying as the intentional, repetitive, or persistent hurting of one person by another, where the relationship involves a perceived imbalance of power.

Bullying can be:

Physical	(kicking, hitting, spitting, taking and/or damaging property or belongings)
Verbal	(threats, teasing, taunting, name-calling, offensive or derogatory remarks)
Indirect	(gossip, spreading negative rumors or stories about someone, lying, excluding people from social groups)
Virtual	(cyber bullying is the term given to sending negative or threatening messages, texts, or pictures via e-mail, IMs, cell phones, chat rooms, or Web sites)

Take Back the Power

Engage the girls in a discussion of ways to respond to bullying behavior.

Ask: *Why do people bully?*

Answers might include:

• Because others do it

• Because it's what you have to do if you want to hang out in certain crowds

• Because it makes them feel stronger, smarter, or better than the person being bullied

• Because it keeps the person who is bullying from being bullied

Ask the girls to name ways they have responded, or seen others respond, to bullying behavior. Answers might include:

• Report it to a teacher, principal, or other adult

• Yell back

• Walk away

• Reason with the bully

• Answer back calmly

• Cry

• Act like it doesn't affect you

Now ask: *Which responses are most effective?* Guide a discussion on the pros and cons of various responses.

Another question to ask: *Why do some kids get teased and others don't?* (Answer: The bully gets pleasure—an "emotional payoff"—from the target's response. So kids who get upset become targets; those who shrug off bullying behavior are left alone.)

Point out that when someone bullies you, your first instinct is to defend yourself—after all, you're being attacked in some way. But research shows that one effective defense, in the moment the bullying is happening, is to show that their insults don't affect you.

Offer up these examples:

Responding defensively against a bully:

Nicole:	*I heard you have a crush on the boys' gym teacher, Mr. Davis, and that you bring him lunch everyday.*
Sophie:	*That's not true!*
Nicole:	*That's what everyone is saying though.*
Sophie:	*They're all big liars! Tell me who started it!*
Nicole:	*I don't know who started it. But everyone knows it's true.*
Sophie:	*It is not true! And you better stop saying it!*

Notice how this conversation can go on and on with Sophie protesting against the rumor. Nicole can continue to needle Sophie, and so, holds the power.

Response to disarm a bully:

Nicole:	*I heard you have a crush on the boys' gym teacher, Mr. Davis, and that you bring him lunch every day.*
Sophie:	*Do you believe it?*
Nicole:	*No.*
Sophie:	*Good.*

Notice there is nothing else Nicole can say about the rumor because Sophie hasn't given any indication that it upsets her.

Alternate response to disarm a bully:

Nicole:	*I heard you have a crush on the boys' gym teacher, Mr. Davis, and that you bring him lunch every day.*
Sophie:	*Do you believe it?*
Nicole:	*Yes.*
Sophie:	*You can believe it if you like.*

Again Nicole is stuck. Sophie is basically asking, "Are you really that gullible?" This makes Nicole's "yes" answer seem ridiculous, which turns the power dynamic in the conversation back to Sophie.

BULLYING: SEE IT ON FILM

The Girl Scout documentary "Sister to Sister: The Darker Side of Friendship" shows how girls use relational aggression in and out of school, and even online, against a new girl who wants to become part of their group. Gossip, rumors, and exclusion, as well as verbal and emotional bullying are seen in the documentary. Girls also talk candidly about friendships and the issues that arise when relationships with boys enter the picture. A series of scenes also compare some of the girls' behaviors with the values of the Girl Scout Law.

You might show the documentary, ask girls do a "scene rewind" with some of the scenarios, and then have a discussion using the points provided above.

Contact your Girl Scout council for the best way to view the documentary.

Flip the Script

Invite girls to break into teams of three and assign each team one of the bullying scenarios on pages 85–87 of their book.

Share with the girls this powerful statistic from the Anti-Bullying Alliance: "Witnesses play a very important role in bullying situations. Bullying will stop in less than 10 seconds nearly 60 percent of the time when peers intervene!" Witnesses (those who observe or are present during bullying) are in a very important position because they can positively or negatively affect the situation. The person who gets bullied is referred to as "target" and not as "victim," because "victim" is disempowering. Also, "target" depersonalizes the bullying.

Explain the activity:

• Decide who will be the bully, witness, and target.

• Use the ideas we have been discussing related to witnesses and taking back the power to "flip the script" so that the bully does not get away with her behavior.

• Try to do your "performance" in the way you think it could work in real life.

• Even though this is serious stuff, you can still get dramatic and have some fun acting it out!

Once the teams have had a chance to figure out and practice "flipping the script," invite them to take turns performing for each other. As each performance ends, invite the "audience" members to offer other suggestions about how they might navigate the situation.

When every team has "flipped the script," wrap up with a team discussion, using questions such as:

• **How can bullies become a roadblock** in the maze of life? What can you do to get around this roadblock?

• **How can you "rewind the scene"** to prevent relationship meltdowns when you're facing a real-life situation where bullying is taking place?

• **How does bullying behavior impact team work?** How could you shift bullying behavior on a team so that everyone can work together successfully?

Surfing Through Cyber Relationships

Transition into a discussion about life online by asking (or welcoming a girl to ask) questions like:

- *What's the weirdest IM or text you ever got?*

- *What's the funniest mass e-mail you ever saw?*

- *Which do you like the most: IMing, texting, or e-mailing? Why?*

- *If you could visit only one Web site for the rest of your life, what would it be and why?*

- *What's your favorite thing to do online?*

Ask girls to share all of the topics they've learned about throughout the aMAZE journey. Ask for a volunteer to write these on a piece of paper the group can look at. Here are the main topics (other may have come up in your group):

- Strengthening friendships
- First impressions and stereotypes
- Peer pressure

- Cliques
- Conflicts
- "I-Statements"

Now ask girls to imagine that all of these relationship topics are taking place in online chat rooms or forums, or through e-mail, IMing, texting, etc.

Divide girls into small teams of two or three. Give each team a sheet of paper and ask them to choose one topic and brainstorm how it "looks, feels, and sounds" online. Here are a few examples:

- **Cliques may "look" like:** girls IMing or texting some girls but excluding others from their conversations or plans.

- **Bullying may "sound" like:** posting a fake Facebook profile or writing mean comments to discussion forums on different sites.

- **Peer pressure may "feel" like:** a girl has to post certain things on her Web page or write e-mails that don't reflect her true opinions.

Then ask the small teams to show and discuss what they wrote. To guide the discussion, ask questions such as:

- *How are relationships or challenging situations different when they occur online? What are some examples of positive and negative risks people are willing to take when they're online?*

- *How do predators, or even peers, lead you into the virtual maze until you reveal more about yourself than you would in a face-to-face interaction? What can you do to prevent this from happening?*

- *E-mailing, IMing, and texting are instantaneous and can feel anonymous. Have you ever written or received hurtful messages or ones that you or others might not say in person? Why does it seem OK online? How does it make you feel?*

- *Do you have friendships that take place mostly online? What "friendship rules" apply to those?*

- *What can you do to promote safety—your own and that of others—online?*

The Girl Scout Law Meets the Virtual World

This activity engages girls in assessing how they interact online. Introduce it by saying something like:

The Girl Scout Law provides a vision and a set of values related to how we ideally want to act in the world. Let's take a look at how you can use the Law as a way to assess some of your online interactions.

Hang up several sheets of newsprint and pass out markers to a few volunteers. Ask girls to look at the Law on the inside front cover of their book and write one or two lines of it at the top of each sheet of newsprint. Then open it up to a free-for-all.

- **The girls can use sticky notes** to write an IM or any online message that somehow relates to the Girl Scout Law—positive or negative. All entries should be anonymous.

- **Play some music while the girls write** and put up their examples. This should be fun but not silly in an off-the-track way.

Ideally, this should result in a visible scene of how broadly the elements of the Law can reach. Here are a few examples:

For honest: "I'm just telling you what she said." For uses resources wisely: "I totally need that pair of shoes in brown, purple, black, AND pink!"

Finish by asking a few questions, such as:

- *Is it hard to stay committed to the Girl Scout Law? Why?*

- *Why does online communication make it easy to forget the Girl Scout Law? (Is it the fact that you can be anonymous?)*

- *How can you use the Law to "increase the peace" in your world?*

TOWARD PEACE

Before the session ends, give girls time (and scraps of paper!) to add to their Peacemaker Kits. Encourage them to consider what they can do about bullying behavior—in their real and virtual worlds—to increase the peace. What have they learned that would make a difference?

LOOKING AHEAD TO SESSION 5

Invite the girls to think about any topics or exercises they would like to explore further at the start of the next session—before they delve into their Take Action Project. (See page 66, "Heading Out of the Maze.")

Preparing for Sessions 5-7

During Session 5, the girls will move from using good relationship skills in their own lives to using their skills to improve relations in the world around them. As they "open out" their mazes, girls will also explore the Girl Scout definition of leadership and see themselves as leaders. Time permitting, though, the group may want to start this session with a few topics and exercises from Sessions 3-4 that they didn't yet get to try.

Planning for the Take Action Project

During Session 5, girls will select and plan a Take Action project that enables them to engage others in using relationship skills to increase the peace. Girls can carry out the Take Action project during Sessions 6 and 7, or, agree to set up time to do it outside of sessions. They may even think of a project they can carry out during the school day, or as part of another group they belong to (a place of worship, a sports team, or club).

As girls plan their Take Action Project, be sure they understand the differences between service and action. The "Service vs. Action" section on the next page can help you guide a discussion with the girls. The Cadettes may not be able to achieve sustainability with their projects but it's still good for them to think about it and strive for it.

Service vs. Action

Service is often the immediate, and much needed, response to a basic need: food, clothing, shelter, care. You are of service when you feed the hungry, offer clothing to the homeless, or simply help a friend with a tough homework assignment. Being of service is a vital way to help and care.

Still, after your good service ends, the people you help are still in need—possibly on a daily basis. What could you do to address those needs in an ongoing way? How could you get to the root of the issue?

Moving Toward Action

When you move beyond immediate service to understand the root causes of a problem, you move toward action. When you team up and mobilize others in your efforts to find ways to solve that problem, you're connecting and taking action.

Service makes the world better for some people "right now." Action makes the world better for more people for the long term. Sometimes, service and action just naturally blend into one sustainable effort. As a Girl Scout, you use both service and action to live by the Girl Scout Law and "make the world a better place."

TOWARD THE DIPLOMAT AWARD

Girls can carry out a Take Action Project on their own or by working with other girls—in large or small teams. To earn the Diplomat Award, girls will go through seven steps of taking action, as shown on page 114 of their book:

- Identify the issue they want to take action on

- Brainstorm a Take Action Project solution

- Assess resources

- Create a plan and time line for specific actions to accomplish the project

- Publicize the Take Action Project

- Carry out the Take Action Project

- Reflect on the results

Scale and Scope of the Take Action Project

You play an important role in coaching girls to choose and plan a project that:

• Is "do-able" in the time they have

• meets a genuine need girls identify in the world around them

• enables girls to use or pass on some of the relationship skills they are experiencing during their aMAZE journey

• engages girls in understanding the difference between "one shot" and "sustainable" and striving toward some degree of sustainability

• will be exciting, fun and meaningful to do and talk about

As you begin to coach girls on the project, lay out up front whatever scheduling, transportation, or other logistical constraints they will have to work around. For example, can the group meet at a different time, date, and location to do the take action? Or, can they design a project that they can do during the school day (using time at their aMAZE meetings to prepare)? Are there other ways to Take Action that the girls can think of?

NO TAKE ACTION PROJECT? PARTNER ON!

If girls are not interested in doing a Take Action Project and earning the Diplomat Award, they can continue to partner with you to organize meetings that engage them in understanding and practicing healthy relationship dynamics.

Sessions 5-7 can easily be built around the optional activities offered at the end of Sessions 1-4. Do invite girls to engage in the leadership activities in Session 5 and encourage them to look at the exercises and topics in their own book that they haven't explored yet as a group and plan to dive into together.

Aim for a mix of active "doing" experiences (role playing, brainstorming exercises, creative projects), discussions that deepen the experience, and reflection time for girls to consider skills to add to their Peacemaker Kits.

Toward Peace: Ideas for Taking Action

Remember, a diplomat uses skill to relate to others. Below are some ideas for girls to consider as they think about how they can share their "amazing skills" with others, creating a "pass it forward" effect. These are just to get girls thinking about all the possibilities. These are not the only things girls could do! Girls will gain the most when they create their own ideas!

- **PASS IT ON:** Girls could choose a role play, activity or discussion that they have participated in on aMAZE (or one they like in their books). They could think about who else in their lives could benefit from doing the same activity. For example, maybe they could get permission to lead a special lunch time (or early morning or after school) session for interested kids at school? Maybe a teacher would even allow this as a classroom activity? Girls could then decide to adjust the activity for their audience.

- **PASS IT DOWN:** Perhaps the Cadettes would like to assist younger girls with their relationship skills and could organize a mini workshop by thinking about how to adjust a few of the activities in aMAZE for younger girls. Maybe it's even a "get ready for middle school" session? Can the Cadettes offer this to younger Girl Scouts or children in elementary school? Perhaps girls could "up the sustainability" factor by leaving behind a "tip sheet" and activity kit that teachers could use to keep the relationship skill building growing in their classrooms.

- **INCREASE ADULT AWARENESS:** Do the Cadettes think adults (teachers, parents, Girl Scout volunteers) could be a little (or a lot!) more savvy about the real relationship issues they are dealing with? Maybe Cadettes want to organize a workshop that allows them to give adults some ideas about how to be more aware of and understanding about the "maze of their lives"? For example, what role can adults play as "witness" to bullying behavior? How could the session end so adults "pass it forward"?

- **SPREAD THE WORD:** Do girls have access to newspapers—local, school, or place of worship or Web sites or radio stations? Do they want to develop a "mini series" or awareness campaign?

- **BUILD A NETWORK:** What resources are available in the community to assist young people with relationship issues? Are there hotlines, conflict mediation projects, safe spaces for kids to hang out together? Are girls interested in a Take Action Project that asks schools or youth centers to create some of these resources?

- **TRADE LESSONS:** Girls could work with a local center for elders to create an annual (or more frequent!) Inter-Generational Tea. Girls and elders trade "lessons learned" in relating with others. Do seniors know what can go wrong with IMing? Do girls know how people interacted before there was the Internet? How might girls and elders increase the peace together based on their information trade?

"Let there be peace on earth
And let it begin with me;
Let there be peace on earth,
The peace that was meant to be."

— Jill Jackson and Sy Miller, "Let There Be Peace on Earth"

SAMPLE SESSION 5
Let Peace Begin with You

AT A GLANCE

Goal: Girls explore the Girl Scout definition of leadership and apply it to their lives, learn how leaders use relationship skills to improve the world, and create and plan a Take Action project to increase the peace in their world

- Opening Ceremony
- How Do Relationship Skills Impact the World?
- Who Is a Real Leader?
- Taking Action on Relationships
- Toward Peace

Opening Ceremony

Invite girls to conduct an opening ceremony of their choice. If they can't think of one, suggest they each share briefly, around the circle, what comes to mind when they hear this quote:

> *I've learned that people will forget what you said, people will forget what you did, but people will never forget how you made them feel.*

> —Maya Angelou

How Do Relationship Skills Impact the World?

Open the discussion by making these points (as always, feel free to use your own words):

- *We've been concentrating on building our own relationship skills—to give us more confidence going through the maze of our own lives.*

- *Today we are going to open our mazes out wider and think about relationships in the whole world around us.*

- *Can you think of examples or stories (from history or the present) about people who use their relationship skills to improve the world? Who? How?*

- *If girls are stuck, remind them they have a few examples in their books.*

- *Can you think of examples or stories about how "bad relationship skills" (like bullying behavior or unresolved conflicts) have contributed to problems in the world?*

Who Is a Real Leader?

Ask the girls to form small groups and make three lists showing a leader's top three personal qualities, skills, and accomplishments.

Then ask all the groups to come together so each small group can share its lists. What do the lists have in common? How do they differ? Ask the full group to create a "master" team definition of a leader's qualities, skills, and accomplishments.

Then, ask if anyone knows the Girl Scout definition of leadership? Refer girls to page 10 of their book for the "Discover, Connect, Take Action" definition of leadership. Ask them to consider how the Girl Scout definition compares to the definition they just came up with on their own. (Hint: If girls get stuck, coach them to look past "word" differences to the deeper meaning. Does leadership have something to do with who you are, how you interact with others, and how you act in the world?)

Ask girls to take a quiet few minutes to think about the qualities, skills, and accomplishments that define them personally as leaders.

Taking Action on Relationships

Invite the girls to share what they have just written with the larger group or in small groups.

Then, say something like: You have the chance to demonstrate your leadership through a Take Action Project that will enable you to advance peace in the world.

With girls sitting comfortably, hang a big piece of paper on the wall. Invite a volunteer to capture the group's ideas. It might be helpful to set up a chart like the one below to guide the brainstorm:

ISSUE AREA	POSSIBLE SOLUTION 1	POSSIBLE SOLUTION 2

Start the discussion by asking:

What topics have we been navigating in aMAZE that we could take out of our group and spread to other girls, our schools, Girl Scouting, or other places we belong?

What issue matters most to you?

If girls are stuck getting started, suggest that they flip through their books to review the various topics:

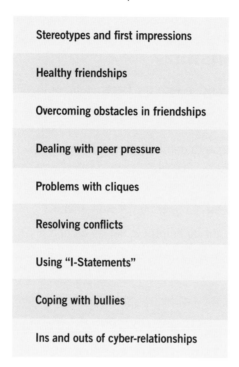

Stereotypes and first impressions

Healthy friendships

Overcoming obstacles in friendships

Dealing with peer pressure

Problems with cliques

Resolving conflicts

Using "I-Statements"

Coping with bullies

Ins and outs of cyber-relationships

If girls are totally stuck when it comes to choosing an issue, share some of the same ideas you have in your book on page 69 and refer them to the ideas in their book on pages 115–119.

Once girls have a general "issue area," even something general such as "healthy relationships," encourage them to add the next layer to their thinking: solutions. In other words, what will they do about their issue area that can make a difference in the world around them? If their issue is "healthy friendships," their solution possibilities might include: teaching younger girls about "true friendships" or holding a "celebrating friendships" series during their school lunch periods.

Reaching a Decision

Encourage the group to brainstorm as many ideas as possible—and not just latch onto the first or "easiest" one that comes to mind. Then, guide the group to come to a decision about an issue they care enough about to address through a Take Action Project. Notice the "rating system" girls have on page 120 of their book and see if they want to try it out.

If the group is large, or girls simply have a hard time choosing, you might also:

- Have the girls form groups of three to review the list of ideas/issues they've collected, and identify two top choices.

- Have each group share their top two, including a quick "pitch" to plug their choice. Have the recorder use tick marks beside the ideas/issues listed on the paper to help the girls visualize any group agreement on a project.

- Ask girls how they want to come to agreement. Majority vote? Come to consensus by continuing to discuss? Compromise and blend ideas? Decide to divvy up and do more than one project?

Planning the Take Action Project

Now that girls know what they want to do to improve relationships in their world, they can jump right in and start planning. Invite them to use the tips and tools in their books to assess their resources (time, people, money), break down the steps they will need to take, and think about their time frame. Encourage them. They may have to adjust their solution as they work through their plans based on what is realistic for them to accomplish.

Toward Peace

Before the session closes, invite girls to reflect on what they can now add to their Peacemaker Kits. (Perhaps something about their role as leaders or ideas for future action projects.)

BEFORE LEAVING aMAZE FOR THE DAY

As the session wraps up, have the team discuss any follow-up steps they can do before the next gathering to bring their Take Action Project to life. Do they need to think of a slogan for an awareness campaign? Or create a skit that would teach younger girls how to respond to a bully? You can also ask the girls what they might like you or other adults to do. They might want adults to initiate some phone calls or help gather information.

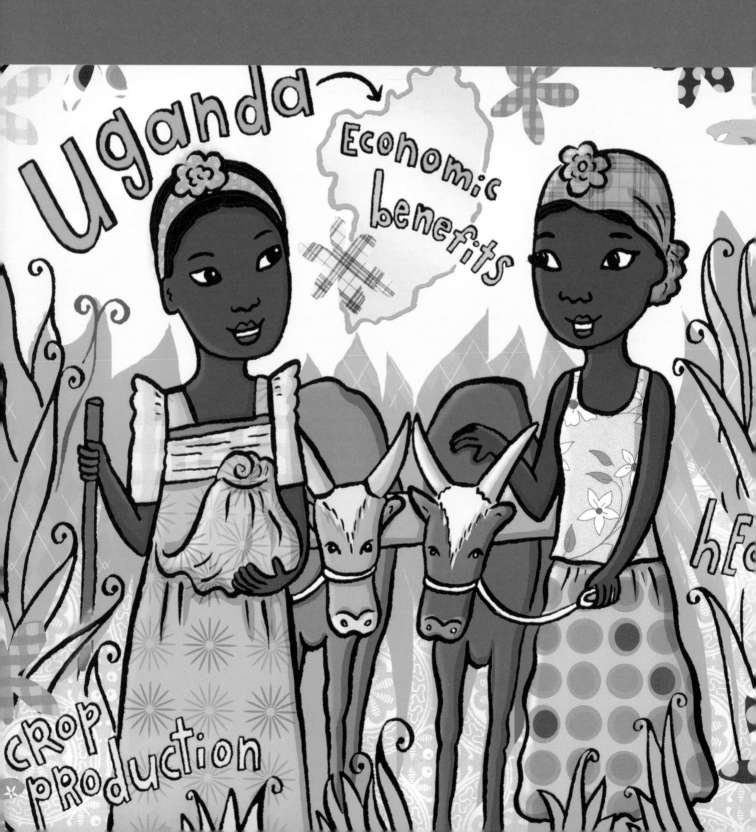

SAMPLE SESSION 6
Improving Relationships in the World

AT A GLANCE

Goal: Girls continue to connect with each other, practicing relationship skills individually and as team members, as they begin to carry out their Take Action Project.

Creating or Doing (a Take Action Project to increase the peace)

Creating or Doing

Depending on the nature of the project girls are doing, they might use this session to create materials (skits, posters, workshops) to share with others. Or they might be out "doing" (talking to school staff about the best three ways to stop the bullying in the halls). Girls can continue following the ideas in their books to develop their projects. If their project involves leading a workshop, they might find pages 124-126 especially useful.

The girls are probably now somewhere between Steps 4 and 6 toward earning their Diplomat Award. While girls are bringing their project to life:

- **Encourage them!**

- **Ask questions to guide them to think about sustainability:** What might they add to their efforts to encourage people to "pass forward" what they learn as a result of the girls' workshop or campaign? Can a school, youth center, or other organization continue some aspect of the project after girls finish? Perhaps make it an annual or quarterly event?

- **Remind girls that they might use some of their aMAZE activities** or discussions as part of their projects. How would they adjust them for other audiences?

- **Take time for girls to reflect** once again about how they're functioning as a team and what they are learning that they can add to their Peacemaker Kits.

- **Assist girls as they organize** some of the practical aspects of their projects by calling on the Family and Friends Network for extra support. Who can drive? Who can pick up posters? Who can help the girls polish their script?

"Winning has always meant much to me, but winning friends has meant the most."

—Babe Didrikson Zaharias

SAMPLE SESSION 7

Toward Peace: Take Action!

AT A GLANCE

Goal: Girls wrap up their Take Action Project and look ahead to their closing celebration and award ceremony.

- **Thinking About the Journey's End**
- **Wrapping Up the Take Action Project**
- **Planning for the Closing Ceremony and Celebration**

Thinking About the Journey's End

As the Take Action Project unfolds and time permits, you might invite the Cadettes to:

• **Discuss the Interact Challenges.** Have those who want to earn the award completed three? What have they learned? How are their efforts being "passed forward?" Girls might enjoy sharing stories about their efforts.

• **Remind the girls about the personal goal(s)** they wrote for themselves and gave to you when they began aMAZE. What insights have they gained that would be useful in accomplishing that goal? Do girls want to get some advice from each other toward accomplishing those goals?

Wrapping Up the Take Action Project

If girls are completing their project, engage the team in discussing what they have learned and accomplished. If not, you can plan to do this as part of the closing (or at a later date if the team has allotted more time for the project).

Here are some questions to guide the discussion:

• *What impact do you think you had? How do you know?*

• *Are there any ways in which your project will be "passed forward"?*

• *What challenges did you face? How did you work around them as a team?*

• *Have you gotten some ideas about other Take Action projects you might want to do toward other Girl Scout Award projects in the future?*

• *What would you want to do differently on other projects?*

• If girls want, they can capture some of their thoughts on page 130 of their book.

• Ask girls who they might need to thank for assisting with or participating in the Take Action Project. *Would they like to write notes, send e-mail messages, or make calls?*

Planning for the Closing Ceremony and Celebration

As the journey through aMAZE nears the end, engage girls in planning a special closing ceremony and celebration. Depending on timing, perhaps they would even like one gathering that is a formal ceremony for their accomplishments, and another that is a team celebration. Either way, here are some ideas to consider:

• Ask girls whether they would like a formal closing ceremony that includes their Family and Friends Network or something just for the team. If they open up the ceremony beyond just the team, maybe some of the people who participated in or helped with the Cadette's Take Action Project might be invited to attend.

• How would girls like to symbolize their "Toward Peace" commitments based on what they have collected in their kits?

• How would girls like to receive the awards they have earned? Do they want a chance to say some special affirmations to one another, acknowledging their efforts and talents they have put into earning the awards?

• How would girls like to honor their accomplishments together? Something fun—maybe a crazy obstacle course-like maze (jump rope, pop balloons, race around chairs) or something quieter—creating a new team poem together or reading through the poems and quotes in their books and talking together about what they mean?

You and the Cadettes might find it useful to flip ahead to Session 8 (here in your guide) and check out some of the "mix and match" ideas provided for the closing. What would make the closing of aMAZE a wonderful event for them?

And, for fun, girls have some ideas in their books, too. So remind them to check page 133 and let you know if they want to incorporate some of these—or do them instead of a more serious closing. Once you have found the way out of the maze, there is no wrong way to exit!

"Ours is a circle of friendships united by ideals."

— Juliette Gordon Low

SAMPLE SESSION 8

Pass It Forward

AT A GLANCE

Goal: Girls reflect on their journey and their personal goals, and commit to expanding peace in their world by using the skills and strategies acquired through aMAZE.

- Opening Ceremony
- Journey Reflection
- Personal Goals
- Thank Yous

- Careers
- Awards
- Closing Ceremony:
  Commitment to Peace

MATERIALS

- Peace Kits
- Awards
- Personal Goals (girls gave you during the first session)

- Any other items needed based on the plans (candles, poems, etc)
- Thank-you notes

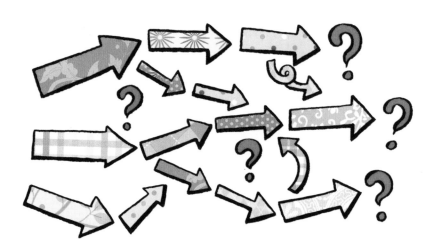

Opening Ceremony

Invite girls to lead an opening they have planned. Perhaps they want to:

• involve guests in a fun ceremony they have enjoyed along the journey?

• use this as an opportunity to read the group poem they created together?

• keep things simple and just enjoy a Friendship Circle?

You might also ask the girls to reflect on this quote from a Kiran, a Girl Guide in Canada:

> *"I try to make this world very peaceful but for that I'm going to need the whole world to help me."*

Journey Reflection

Engage the girls in a final reflection of how they have discovered, connected, and taken action as they have journeyed through the passageways of aMAZE. They can use the reflection on pages 138–139 of their book. Or, if invited guests are present, maybe they want to explain the Girl Scout Leadership Philosophy (Discover, Connect, Take Action) to them?

Personal Goals

Give each girl back her sealed envelope with the goal(s) she wrote during the first session in aMAZE. As you do so, say something special about what the girl has contributed to or accomplished in the passageways of aMAZE. Here are some examples:

_____used her talent for _____to make sure our Take Action Project _____

_____used her humor to help us through emotional conversations.

_____showed us how to _____

When all girls have received their envelopes give them some quiet time to think about how they progressed toward their goal(s). If girls want, they may discuss their insights!

CUSTOMIZE THE CLOSING

Given the variety of activities suggested, mix and match to create a session based on how the girls want to close out the journey. Perhaps they'll start the closing with just their team, and then open the gathering up to family and friends. Just be sure to save time for the girls to reflect on and celebrate their accomplishments and commit to continued efforts to pass peace forward!

Thank Yous

Who would the girls like to thank? (Out loud or by taking time to write a note!)

Careers

Girls might also like to talk about how some of the notable women featured in their books (or others they know of) have used relationship skills to increase the peace. Who inspired them most? Do they see an "increase the peace" career in their futures?

Awards

Engage girls in presenting each other with the awards they have earned along the journey. Encourage them to make this meaningful by talking about what they learned in striving toward the award. Perhaps girls can go around their circle, offering affirmations to each other. What qualities and skills do they admire in each other? Now is the time to offer these gifts out loud. Perhaps girls also want to sign each other's books?

Interact Award: for girls who have completed three of the nine "Interact Challenges" in an effort to advance peace in the world around them—one interaction at a time.

Diplomat Award: for girls who have passed on their relationship skills to others through the seven steps of the Take Action Project.

Peacemaker Award: for girls who have participated in "Toward Peace" reflections by identifying and collecting "tools" and committing to use them throughout their lives to create more peace in the world.

EXTRAS

PEACE Poem

Girls can create a group "PEACE" poem by using the word's five letters to start each line of the poem.

One Last Maze

When they started the journey, girls created mazes to represent the obstacles they navigate in their lives. Maybe they can journey forward together by working in pairs (or threes) to create a maze that shows the start (Me+You) and the end (World Peace). Draw what goes in between.

Plant a Peace Garden

Girls can plant grass seed in a shallow container to symbolically represent their commitment to sow peace. They might also write a quote or other peace message on a paper tag, tie it to a twig, and stick it in the container. Caring for their peace gardens will be a reminder to nurture peaceful thoughts and actions.

Closing Ceremony: Commitment to Peace

Invite each girl to choose one note that she has placed in her Peacemaker Kit and share with the team why that is the most important thing she has gained on the journey through aMAZE. How will she use it to "increase the peace" in her life—and the world around her.

You might also guide the girls to a discussion of Mohandas K. Gandhi, one of the world's most influential peacemakers. Perhaps share this quote from Annie, a Girl Scout Senior from North Carolina:

"The leader I admire most is Gandhi. Because he knew what his goals were and he was able to lead people through peace and avoid what everybody thought was inevitable, which was all this violence. That was the ultimate leadership."

Ask the girls how much they know of Gandhi and his views and actions. Depending on their answers, you might explain that Gandhi believed people should show forgiveness to one another and use positive actions to make up for any less-than-positive acts they have committed. One of Gandhi's most quoted lines is: "You must be the change you wish to see in the world." Ask the girls to say one change they wish to see in the world. *As peacemakers, how will they be this change?*

Next, ask all the girls to stand in a circle. Each, in turn, holds a meaningful symbol (peace sign charm, candle, pebble, olive branch) in her hand as she offers her commitment for peace to herself, and to her sister peacemakers: "I commit to being a peacemaker in the world by _____ ."

After the ceremony and celebration ends, take some time for yourself. Look back at the reflection on page 24–25. Have any of your answers changed since winding through aMAZE?

_____

_____

_____

How do you commit to being a peacemaker?

_____

_____

_____